MAROON 5
HANDS ALL OVER

ISBN 978-1-6177-4038-1

HAL•LEONARD®
CORPORATION
7777 W. BLUEMOUND RD. P.O. BOX 13819 MILWAUKEE, WI 53213

Visit Hal Leonard Online at
www.halleonard.com

MISERY

Words by ADAM LEVINE
Music by ADAM LEVINE, JESSE CARMICHAEL
and SAM FARRAR

Moderate Funk Rock groove

Oh, yeah. _____ Oh,

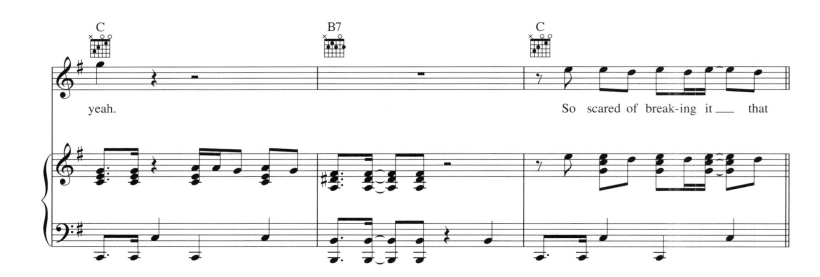

yeah. So scared of break-ing it _____ that

you won't let it bend, _____ and I wrote two hun-dred let-ters
mix-es in with mine, _____ the way it feels to be com-

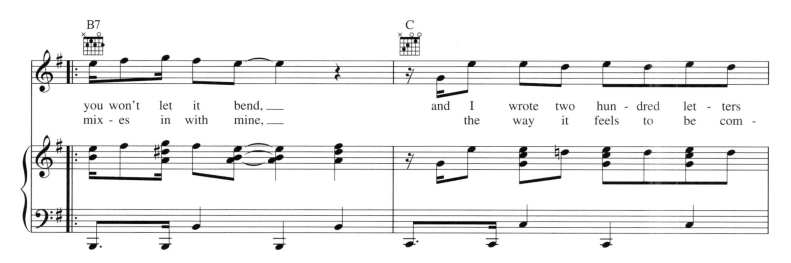

GIVE A LITTLE MORE

Words by ADAM LEVINE
Music by ADAM LEVINE,
JESSE CARMICHAEL and JAMES VALENTINE

With a groove

Now you've been __ bad __ and it goes __ on __

__ and on __ and on __ 'til you come home, __ babe, _

STUTTER

Words by ADAM LEVINE
Music by ADAM LEVINE,
MATT FLYNN and SAM FARRAR

DON'T KNOW NOTHING

Words by ADAM LEVINE
Music by ADAM LEVINE
and SAM FARRAR

With energy

Ooh. _____ Ooh. _____

Liv - ing in - side my head, pull - ing my strings,

let - ting me think I'm in con - trol. Giv - ing you all of my

I _____ don't want to be, I _____ don't want to be _____ a - lone. _____

Ooh. _____ Ooh. _____

Ooh. _____

Optional Ending

Repeat and Fade

Ooh. _____ Ooh. _____

NEVER GONNA LEAVE THIS BED

Words by ADAM LEVINE
Music by ADAM LEVINE

I CAN'T LIE

Words by ADAM LEVINE
Music by ADAM LEVINE
and SAM FARRAR

Moderate groove

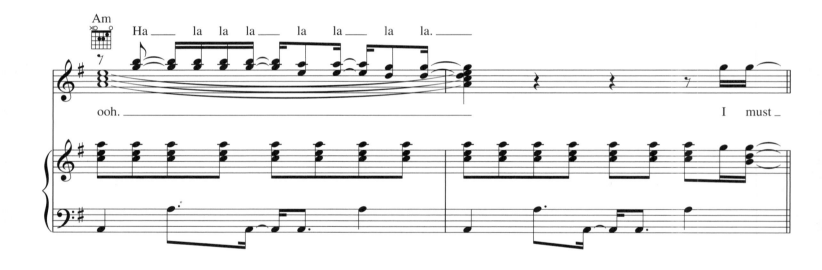

HANDS ALL OVER

Words by ADAM LEVINE
Music by ADAM LEVINE,
JESSE CARMICHAEL and SAM FARRAR

Moderate Funk

HOW

Words by ADAM LEVINE
Music by ADAM LEVINE, JESSE CARMICHAEL,
SHAWN TELLEZ and SAM FARRAR

In solid 4

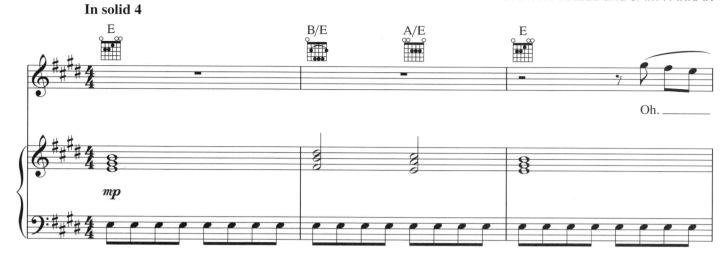

Oh. _____

_____ I've been search-ing for your touch, un-like an-y touch I've

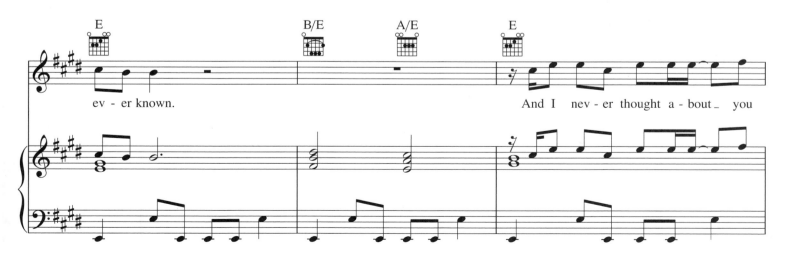

ev-er known. And I nev-er thought a-bout _ you

GET BACK IN MY LIFE

Words by ADAM LEVINE
Music by ADAM LEVINE,
JESSE CARMICHAEL and JAMES VALENTINE

Funk Rock

Ooh, _____ ooh. _____

You are re-lent-less, I am de-fence-less, why did you
Don't rep-ri-mand me, you're so de-mand-ing, but I've got

knock me down to-night? _____ You beat me sense-less, I
time, I don't mind at all. _____ You're pic-ture per-fect, com-

tired, I'll nev-er be__ free, all night, don't fight the feel - ing.

Get back in my life,__ come knock on my door,__ what I'm look-ing for,__

__ I think you should know.__ You've start - ed a__ fire,__

To Coda

__ burned me to the floor.__ Please, don't re - sist an - y - more,__

I'll nev-er leave you a-lone. _____ Ooh, _____

Lead vocal ad lib.

ooh. _____

Ooh, _____ ooh. _____

Repeat and Fade | **Optional Ending**

JUST A FEELING

Words by ADAM LEVINE
Music by ADAM LEVINE
and JESSE CARMICHAEL

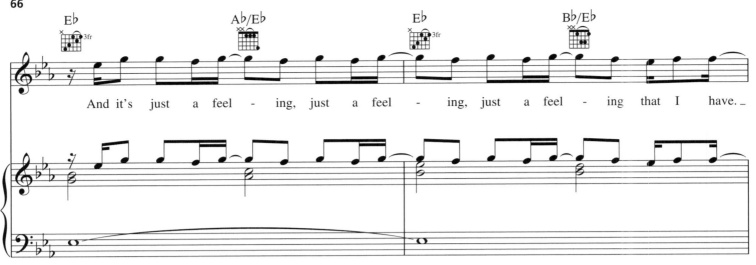

And it's just a feel - ing, just a feel - ing, just a feel - ing that I have. _

Just a feel - ing, just a feel - ing that I have. _

It's _ just a feel -

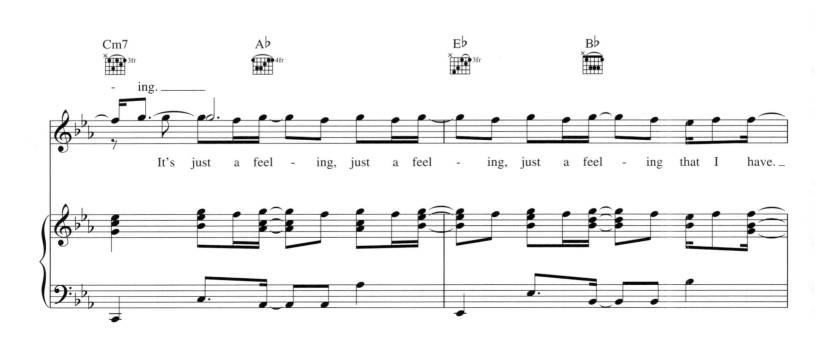

- ing. _____

It's just a feel - ing, just a feel - ing, just a feel - ing that I have. _

RUNAWAY

Words by ADAM LEVINE
Music by ADAM LEVINE,
NOAH PASSOVOY and SAM FARRAR

What am I s'posed to do with this time? ___ It tears so

man-y holes, ___ I stay a-float, but I ___ feel out

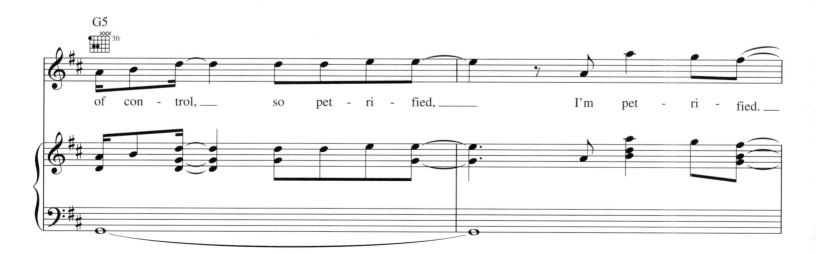

of con-trol, ___ so pet-ri-fied, ___ I'm pet-ri-fied. ___

OUT OF GOODBYES

Words by ADAM LEVINE
Music by ADAM LEVINE,
JESSE CARMICHAEL and JAMES VALENTINE

Calypso feel

Tell me ac - tions speak loud - er,
Nev - er asked you to change, __

but there's some - thing a - bout her __ words __
but __ sad - ly you don't feel the __ same __

that hurt. __
a - bout me. __